Table of C

a 2-3	Day by Day 55
b 4-5	Number Your Paper 56
c 6-7	Terrific Teens 57
d 8-9	Super Tens 58
e 10-11	Check It Out 59
.... 12-13	Vitalizing Veggies 60
g 14-15	Interesting Animal Names 61
h 16-17	Welcome! 62
.... 18-19	Steamboating the Mississippi 63
.... 20-21	Top Ten Best Sellers 64
k 22-23	Current Currency 65
.... 24-25	Submerge into a Sub 66
m 26-27	Dinosaurs by the Dozen 67
n 28-29	Take Good Care Of It! 68
o 30-31	Waffle Cone Masterpieces 69
p 32-33	Where in the World? 70
q 34-35	Final Game Scoreboard 71
.... 36-37	Thirst-Quenching Taste Test 72
.... 38-39	Super Snack 73
.... 40-41	What Am I? 74
u 42-43	Good and Easy! 75
v 44-45	A "Tasty" Riddle 76
w 46-47	Confused Comet 77
x 48-49	Be Creative! 78
y 50-51	It's Your Choice! 79
.... 52-53	**Answer Key** 80
Through the Year 54	

Aa

ABSOLUTELY ATROCIOUS.

A a

a a

A a

Alaska

Alvin

Anna

armadillo

alligator

accordion

afar

amaze

any

appetite

Aa

Alligators accelerate automated autos.

Active alarms abruptly awaken aardvarks.

Bb

Bb

bb

Bb

Barcelona

Brad

Bethany

beaver

bear

bowling

babble

buggy

blink

bib

Bb

Big binoculars
bewilder badgers.

Busy beavers build
brick bridges.

Cc

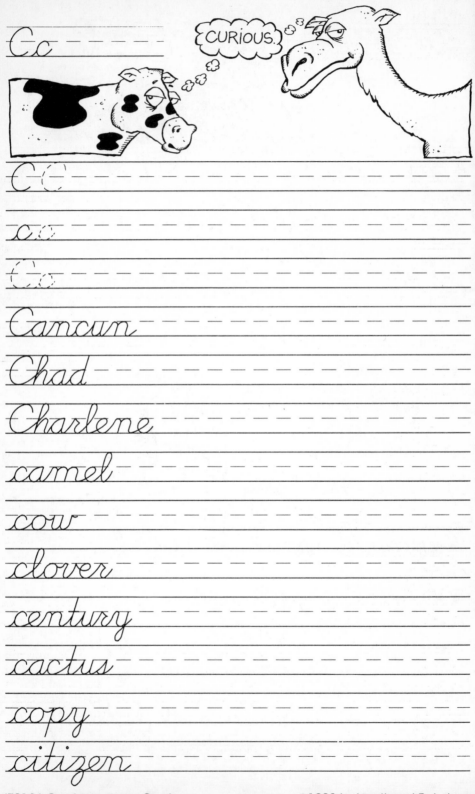

CC

cc

Cc

Cancun

Chad

Charlene

camel

cow

clover

century

cactus

copy

citizen

$\mathcal{C}c$

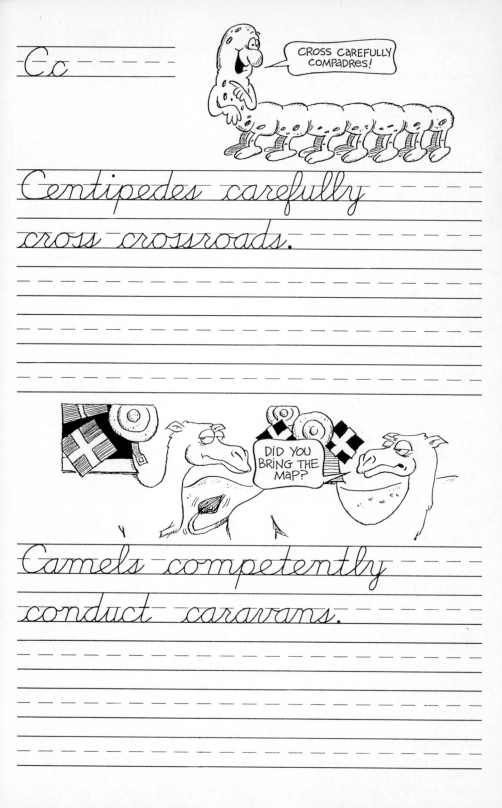

Centipedes carefully
cross crossroads.

Camels competently
conduct caravans.

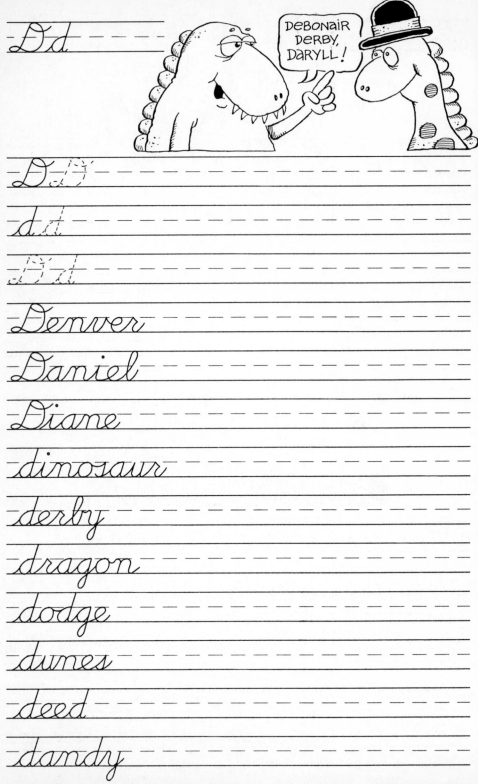

Dd

DD

dd

Dd

Denver

Daniel

Diane

dinosaur

derby

dragon

dodge

dunes

deed

dandy

Dd

Doubtful dinosaurs
dodge double doors.

Dependable dolphins
design docks.

Ee

Ee

e

E

England

Elmer

Elisha

eels

elephant

envelope

eggshells

every

extra

empire

Ee

*Elephant's ears
easily eavesdrop.*

*Every eel emits
electrifying energy.*

Ff

F

f

Ff

Fairbanks

Felix

Fay

fish

flood

fancy

feast

fluffy

fresh

fumble

Ff

FLYING FIRST-CLASS FEELS FABULOUS!

Fireflies frequently fly first-class.

Frazzled frogs furiously fix floats.

$\mathcal{G}\mathcal{g}$

Gee George, a gigantic gumball!

$\mathcal{G}$

$\mathcal{g}$

Granada

Gregory

Gloria

goose

giggle

gumball

gigantic

graph

glacier

gentle

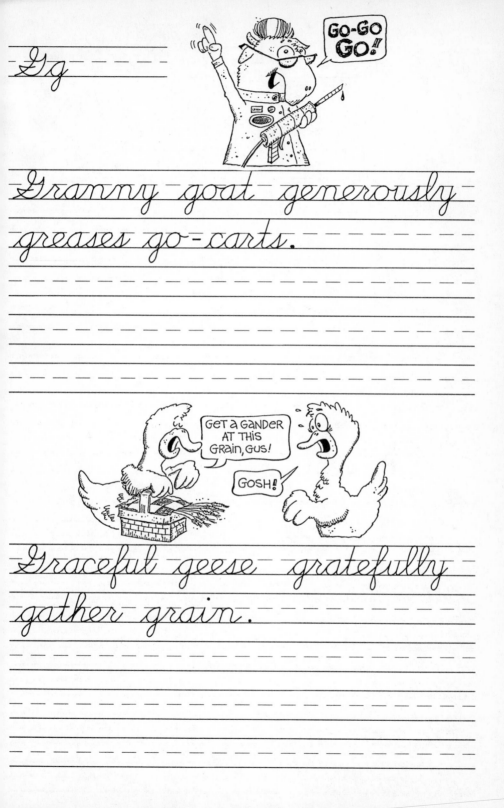

Gg

Granny goat generously greases go-carts.

Graceful geese gratefully gather grain.

Hh

H H

h h

h h

Helsinki

Henry

Hilda

hog

harmonica

hippo

helmet

hurrah

hiccup

highway

Hh

Hefty hippos hail
hovering helicopters.

Honeybees have
honeycombed hotels.

I i

I i

i i

i i

Iowa

Ivan

Irene

itch

insect

inchworm

invisible

imitate

icy

iron

Ii

Intelligent insects
ink invitations.

Inchworms inhabit
isolated islands.

Jj

Jj

jj

jj

Jacksonville

Jeff

Julie

jellyfish

jingle

jewels

juice

jacket

joke

junior

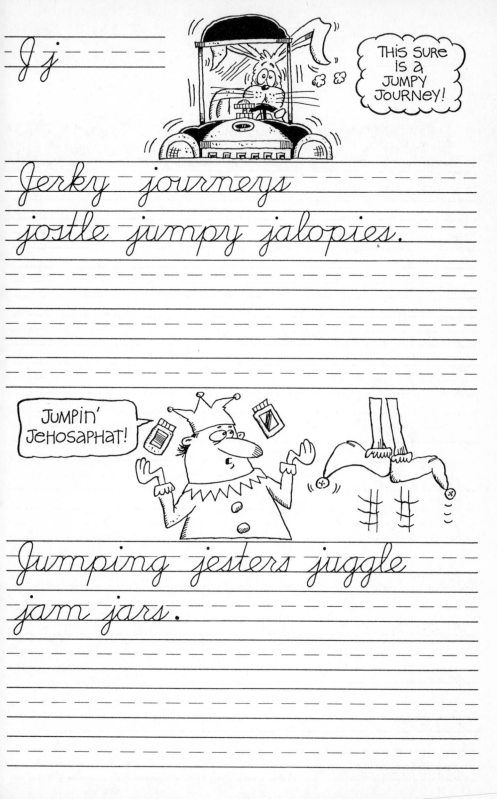

Jj

Jerky journeys

jostle jumpy jalopies.

Jumping jesters juggle

jam jars.

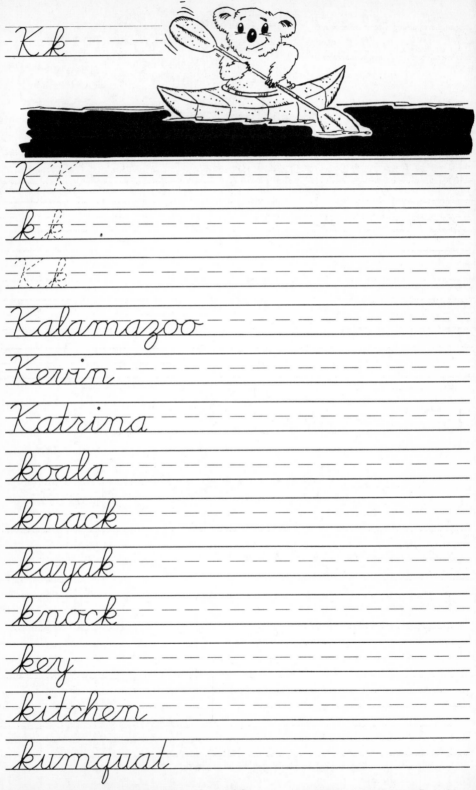

Kk

K K

k k

Kk

Kalamazoo

Kevin

Katrina

koala

knack

kayak

knock

key

kitchen

kumquat

Kk

Kangaroos know
knockout kicks.

Kind koalas knit
khaki kneesocks.

$\mathscr{L} l$

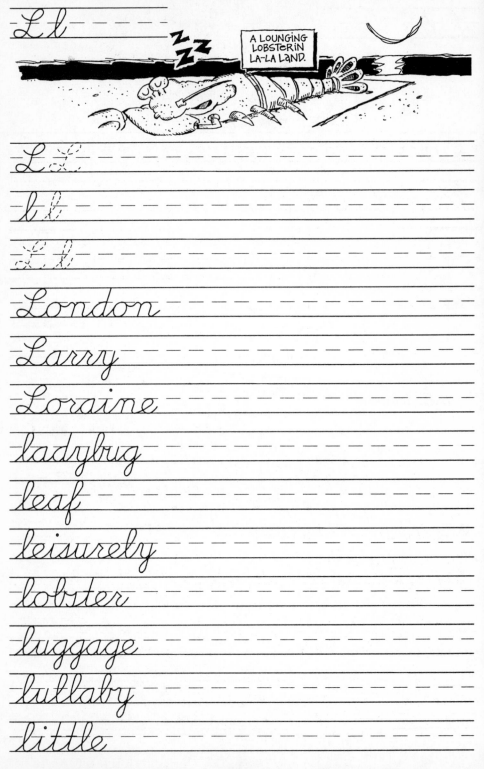

A LOUNGING LOBSTER in LA-LA LAND.

$\mathscr{L}$

$l l$

$\mathscr{L} l$

London

Larry

Loraine

ladybug

leaf

leisurely

lobster

luggage

lullaby

little

Ll

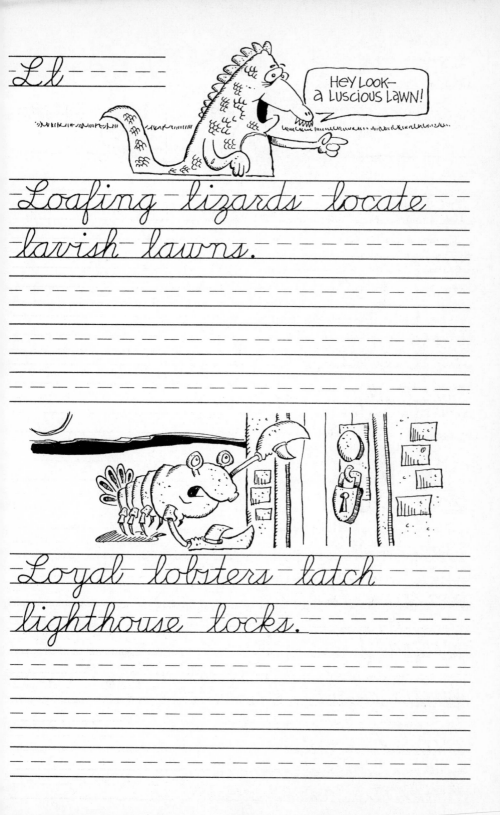

Loafing lizards locate lavish lawns.

Loyal lobsters latch lighthouse locks.

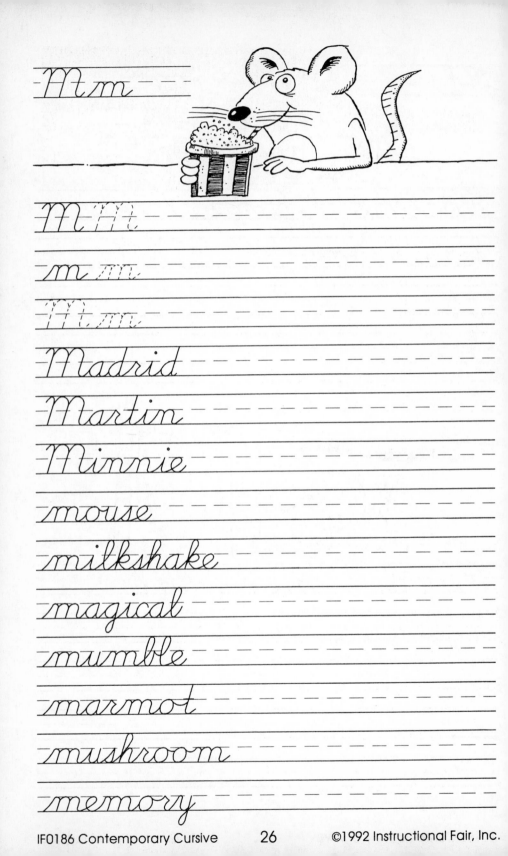

Mm

M M

m m

M m

Madrid

Martin

Minnie

mouse

milkshake

magical

mumble

marmot

mushroom

memory

Mm

Muddled Martians

miss moon missions.

Moose munch

mulberry muffins.

Nn

MY NiCKNAME
iS NiCKY!
NiCKY THE NEWT,
YUP-THAT'S ME!

Nn

nn

Nn

Nottingham

Nate

Norma

newt

notebook

nickname

newspaper

nuisance

napkin

nominate

An

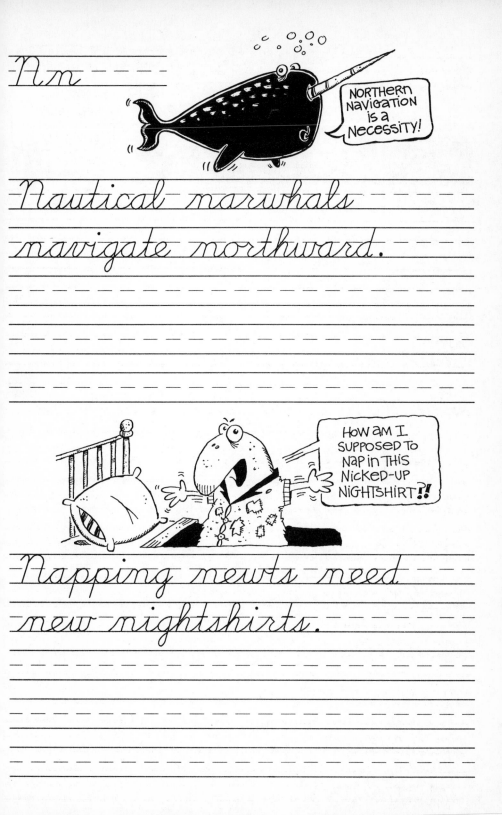

Nautical narwhals navigate northward.

Napping newts need new nightshirts.

Oo

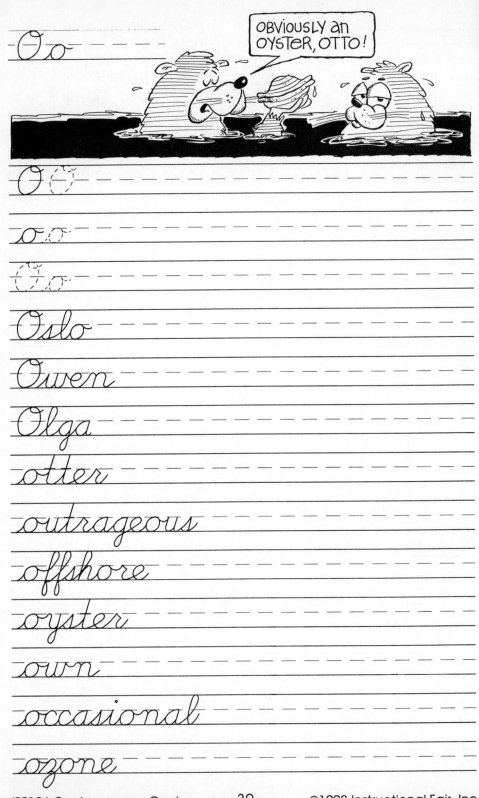

Oo

Oo

Oo

Oslo

Owen

Olga

otter

outrageous

offshore

oyster

own

occasional

ozone

$\mathcal{O}o$

Olympic orangutans
often overact.

Outstanding otter
outrows octopus.

Pp

PERFECT.

P P

p p

Pp

Portugal

Patrick

Peggy

porpoise

prepare

popcorn

peppermint

plump

puppet

parachute

Pp

Portly pigs prefer popped popcorn.

Pensive penguins proofread printouts.

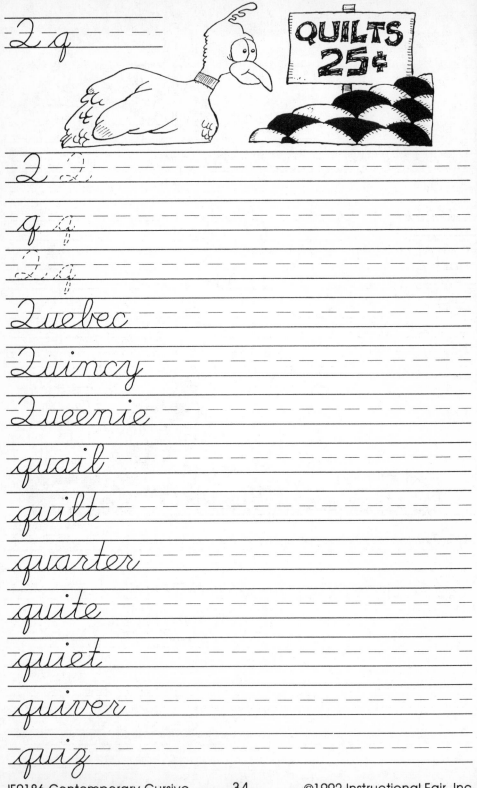

2 q

2 q

q q

Q q

Quebec

Quincy

Queenie

quail

quilt

quarter

quite

quiet

quiver

quiz

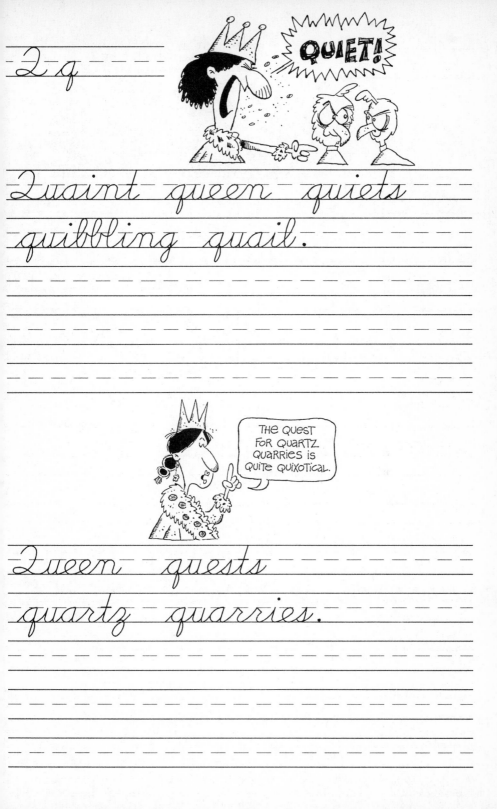

2 q

Quaint queen quiets
quibbling quail.

Queen quests
quartz quarries.

Rr

R R

r r

Rr

Rochester

Ray

Rhonda

raccoon

required

raspberries

robot

ringmaster

runner

roaring

Rr

Racing rabbits require refreshments.

Reliable robots repair ragged rainbows.

$\mathcal{S}\ \mathit{s}$

$\mathcal{S}$

s

$\mathcal{S}\ s$

Spain

Scott

Susanna

starfish

sailing

seashore

scientist

sweatshirt

signs

sherbet

S s

Spunky spiders
somersault slowly.

Snorkeling seals
search shipwrecks.

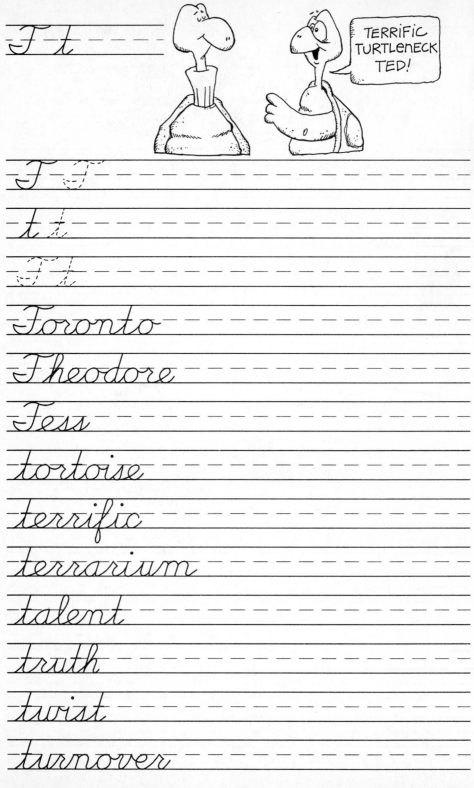

Tt

TERRIFIC TURTLENECK TED!

T T

t t

Tt

Toronto

Theodore

Tess

tortoise

terrific

terrarium

talent

truth

twist

turnover

$\mathcal{T} t$

Talkative toucans try tropical treats.

Tiny tadpoles tackle tricky tides.

Uu

U U

u u

Uu

Uruguay

Uri

Ulysses

uniform

usher

unicorn

usual

update

uranium

ukulele

U u

Unobserving unicorns
upset urchins.

Umpires utter
unpopular ultimatums.

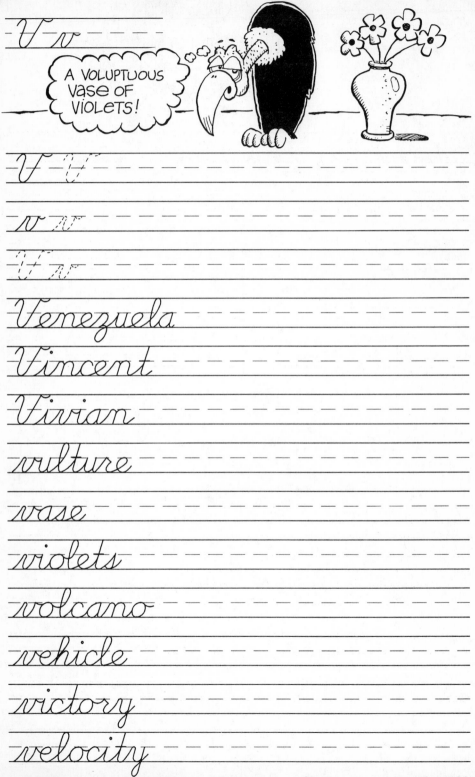

V v

A VOLUPTUOUS
VASE OF
VIOLETS!

V V

v v

V v

Venezuela

Vincent

Vivian

vulture

vase

violets

volcano

vehicle

victory

velocity

Vv

Visitors vocalize volleyball victory.

Voyaging Vikings value vegetables.

Ww

Dear
Winnefred,

W W

w w

Ww

Winnipeg

Wally

Winnie

walrus

wobbly

wharf

westward

willow

write

wonderful

Ww

I WATCH WHIRLING WHIRLPOOLS ON WEDNESDAYS!

Woozy weasels watch whirling waterfalls.

Working woodpeckers whittle wide wedges.

Xx

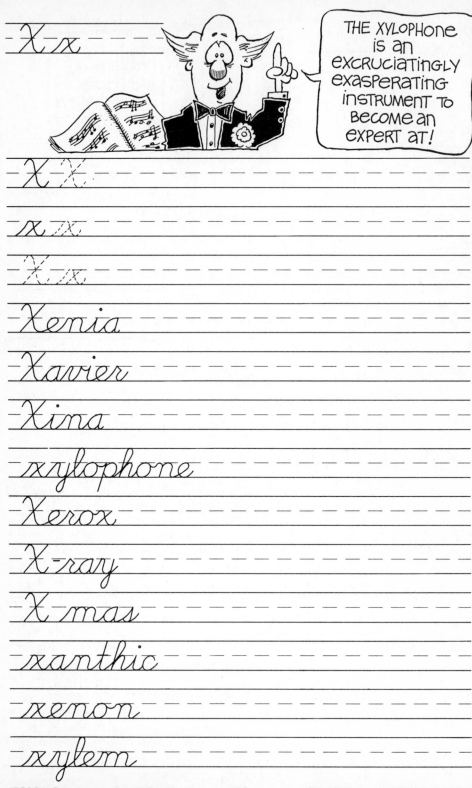

THE XYLOPHONE is an EXCRUCIATINGLY exasperating instrument to become an expert at!

X X

x x

X x

Xenia

Xavier

Xina

xylophone

Xerox

X-ray

X-mas

xanthic

xenon

xylem

_Xx_

Xavier x-rayed

xerophilous xylem.

Xina xeroxes

xanthic xylophones.

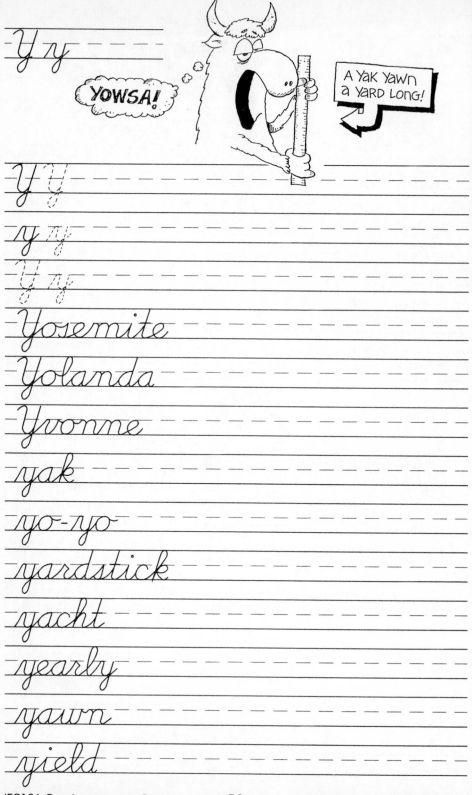

Yy

Yy

y y

Yy

Yosemite

Yolanda

Yvonne

yak

yo-yo

yardstick

yacht

yearly

yawn

yield

Yy

Youngsters yell,
"Yeah! Yearbooks!"

Youthful yaks yacht
yearlong.

I'M NOT a SKUNK, I'M a ZORILLE! HEY PaL-LOOK IT UP!

$\mathscr{Z}$ $\mathscr{z}$

$\mathscr{Z}$ $\mathscr{Z}$

$\mathscr{Z}$ $\mathscr{Z}$

$\mathscr{Z}$ $\mathscr{Z}$

Zanzibar

Zeus

Zurich

zorille

zucchini

zigzag

zoology

zephyr

zone

zipper

Z z

Zephyrs zoom zestfully.

ZOUNDS!

GROUND ZERO, GET IT? AM I A ZANY ZEBRA OR WHAT?

Zealous zebras zigzagged zeros.

All Through the Year

Trace the months of the year. Then write them on the lines.

January _____

February _____

March _____

April _____

May _____

June _____

July _____

August _____

September _____

October _____

November _____

December _____

Day by Day

Take Life one Day at a Time.

Trace and write.

Sunday

Monday

Tuesday

Wednesday

Thursday

Friday

Saturday

Number Your Paper

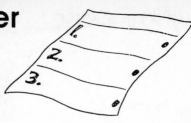

Trace and write the numerals and number words.

0 zero

1 one

2 two

3 three

4 four

5 five

6 six

7 seven

8 eight

9 nine

10 ten

Terrific Teens

So I'm, um, like at the mall, y'know, and I'm like shopping and everything and stuff...

Trace and write the numerals and number words.

11 eleven

12 twelve

13 thirteen

14 fourteen

15 fifteen

16 sixteen

17 seventeen

18 eighteen

19 nineteen

20 twenty

Super Tens

Trace and write the numerals and number words.

10 ten

20 twenty

30 thirty

40 forty

50 fifty

60 sixty

70 seventy

80 eighty

90 ninety

100 one hundred

Check It Out

Look at the completed check. Then fill in the missing information on the check at the bottom.

Jack Smith No. 1245
2560 W. Axle
Garage, Ohio 97260

April 29, 1991

Pay To the
Order of *Ann Jones* **$ 7.35**

Seven and 35/100 Dollars

Memo *frisbee* *Jack Smith*

Jack Smith No. 1245
2560 W. Axle
Garage, Ohio 97260

Pay To the
Order of $

Dollars

Memo

Vitalizing Veggies

Find and circle the names of fourteen vegetables.
Then write them on the lines.

v	p	o	t	a	t	o	e	i	e	g	l	s	c
c	a	c	u	c	u	m	b	e	r	o	e	u	a
e	a	s	p	a	r	a	g	u	s	g	t	b	r
l	o	y	e	c	c	o	r	n	e	t	t	e	r
e	a	r	t	u	r	n	i	p	y	a	u	e	o
r	t	c	a	b	b	a	g	e	d	o	c	t	t
y	d	e	o	r	a	d	i	s	h	e	e	r	v
v	s	e	c	a	u	l	i	f	l	o	w	e	r
f	z	u	c	c	h	i	n	i	r	t	i	m	i
b	r	o	c	c	o	l	i	a	y	n	a	h	m

------ ------
------ ------
------ ------
------ ------
------ ------
------ ------
------ ------

60

nteresting Animal Names

HEY-WHAT ABOUT FROGS?
FROGS ARE INTERESTING TOO!

Write the names of the animals in alphabetical order.

jaguar	wapiti	manatee
wallaby	chameleon	wombat
mongoose	zebu	tapir
vicuña	whippet	sloth

1.

2.

3.

4.

5.

6.

7.

8.

9.

10.

11.

12.

Welcome!

Write the years and names of the states in order beginning with the first state to become part of the United States.

Illinois -1818   Michigan -1837   Ohio -1803
Indiana -1816   Minnesota -1858   Oregon -1859
Iowa -1846   Missouri -1821   South Dakota -1889
Kansas -1861   Nebraska -1867   Wisconsin -1848

Steamboating the Mississippi

Follow the steamboat ride down the Mississippi River. Write the names of the towns in the order that the steamboat passes by them.

RT • Hannibal

• St. Louis

Cape Girardeau •

•Cairo

New Madrid

Memphis

•Greenville

•Vicksburg

•Natchez

Baton Rouge

Nottoway

• New Orleans •

nisH

Top Ten Best Sellers

Write the titles of the ten books you like best from this list.

Charlotte's Web
The Phantom Tollbooth
Superfudge
Tuck Everlasting
Freckle Juice
Amelia Bedelia

Pippi Longstocking
The Return of the Indian
Julie and the Wolves
The Cay
Soup
Iggie's House
Bunnicula

Current Currency

Draw a line to match the country to the name of its currency. Then write the country and its currency on the lines.

United States	yen	England	mark
Mexico	dollar	Germany	pound
Japan	peso	Italy	cruzeiro
Denmark	franc	Brazil	drachma
France	krone	Greece	lira

Submerge into a Sub

Write a list of the nine ingredients you would use to create your own sub sandwich.

mustard	pizza sauce	lettuce
tomato	onion	pickles
turkey	peppers	ham
ketchup	salami	cheese
mushrooms	bologna	olives
meatballs	mayonnaise	

1.

2.

3.

4.

5.

6.

7.

8.

9.

What would you name your submarine sandwich?

Dinosaurs by the Dozen

Write the names of the dinosaurs in alphabetical order.

tyrannosaurus   archaeopteryx   pteranodon
ophthalmosaurus   diplodocus   ankylosaurus
parasaurolophus   ichthyosaur   dimetrodon
stegosaurus   hesperornis   triceratops

1. _____

2. _____

3. _____

4. _____

5. _____

6. _____

7. _____

8. _____

9. _____

10. _____

11. _____

12. _____

Take Good Care Of It!

Find and circle the names of eighteen parts of the body. Then write them on the lines.

a	h	e	a	d	a	f	o	o	t	h	e	y	e
r	n	e	c	k	m	o	u	t	h	i	o	l	t
m	n	e	y	e	b	r	o	w	g	p	t	e	o
v	o	w	r	i	s	t	o	h	n	k	o	g	k
m	s	e	s	h	o	u	l	d	e	r	e	d	n
w	e	c	h	i	n	a	n	k	l	e	a	v	e
e	a	r	h	a	f	i	n	g	e	r	e	m	e

Waffle Cone Masterpieces

Write ten ingredients you would use to make a
waffle cone.

yogurt   coconut   blueberries
ice cream   cookie pieces   strawberries
chocolate syrup   chocolate chips   peanuts
caramel syrup   candy pieces   whipped cream
marshmallow   cherries

1. _____

2. _____

3. _____

4. _____

5. _____

6. _____

7. _____

8. _____

9. _____

10. _____

Where in the World?

Write the name of each country under the correct heading.

Argentina   China   Soviet Union   Spain

Costa Rica   Norway   Panama   Chile

New Zealand   Uruguay   Mexico   Fiji

South Africa   Bolivia   Paraguay   Peru

Australia   England   United States   Canada

Northern Hemisphere	**Southern Hemisphere**

Final Game Scoreboard

Write the names of the teams in order beginning
with the team that won the most games.

Team	Wins	Team	Wins
Knights	10	Seafarers	5
Ranchers	7	Skyriders	11
Foresters	4	Winders	2
Steamers	12	Miners	15
Pledges	3	Harvesters	9

1. _____

2. _____

3. _____

4. _____

5. _____

6. _____

7. _____

8. _____

9. _____

10. _____

Thirst-Quenching Taste Test

The graph shows how many people chose each beverage as their favorite. Write the names of the beverages in order beginning with the most popular.

Beverage	Number of People (1 square = 5 people)
apple juice	
chocolate milk	
cranberry juice	
hot chocolate	
ice-cream soda	
iced tea	
lemonade	
milk	
milkshake	
orange juice	
soda pop	
water	

1. _____

2. _____

3. _____

4. _____

5. _____

6. _____

7. _____

8. _____

9. _____

10. _____

11. _____

12. _____

Super Snack

Copy the recipe. Then enjoy your snack!

1 rice cake   peanut butter
margarine   honey

Spread margarine on top of the rice cake. Then spread on some peanut butter. Finally spread honey on top.

What Am I?

HEY DUDE—
I Know!

Copy and solve the riddle.

I can be one color or have a very bright design.
I can move fast or slow. People can stand on me
with one or both feet. I can leap high or low. I have
a board and four wheels. What am I?

I am a _____ .

Good and Easy!

Copy the recipe. Then try it!

2 cups chocolate chips

1 tablespoon shortening

5 cups rice cereal

1 cup chopped walnuts

Melt chocolate chips and shortening over low heat. Stir until smooth. Pour over cereal and nuts. Mix well. Drop by teaspoons onto waxed paper. Refrigerate for 1 hour. Eat and enjoy!

A "Tasty" Riddle

Copy and solve the riddle.

IT'S PREFERRED BY PORTLY PORKERS!

Indians discovered me hundreds of years ago. I am usually white or yellow, but can be various other colors. People like to eat me for a treat at the movies. When I am heated, I change size and shape. I taste terrific with butter and salt. What am I? I am _____ .

Confused Comet

Unscramble each set of words to make a sentence.
Then write each sentence on the lines.

1. huge resembles A a comet snowball.

2. millions length. in miles The be tail of can

3. the melts The heat sun's layer of outer ice.

4. Bits escape of to and gases form dust tail. the

1. _____

_____

_____

2. _____

_____

_____

3. _____

_____

_____

4. _____

_____

_____

77

Be Creative!

Choose one word from each list (A, B, C and D) to create your own sentences. Write your sentences on the lines.

A

Gigantic
Strange
Daring
Speedy

B

elephants
dinosaurs
skateboarders
windsurfers

C

jumped
roamed
leaped
trampled

D

waves.
the earth.
ramps.
the jungle.

1.

2.

3.

4.

It's Your Choice!

Choose one word from each list (A, B, C and D) to create your own sentences. Write your sentences on the lines.

A	B
Colorful	giraffes
Soaring	automobiles
Roaring	hang gliders
Graceful	sailboards

C	D
fly	high above the ground.
sail	over the tall fence.
race	past the checkered flag.
stretch	against the current.

1.

2.

3.

4.

Answer Key

Page 60

Page 61

1. chameleon
2. jaguar
3. manatee
4. mongoose
5. sloth
6. tapir
7. vicuña
8. wallaby
9. wapiti
10. whippet
11. wombat
12. zebu

Page 62

Ohio – 1803
Indiana – 1816
Illinois – 1818
Missouri – 1821
Michigan – 1837
Iowa – 1846
Wisconsin – 1848
Minnesota — 1858
Oregon – 1859
Kansas – 1861
Nebraska – 1867
South Dakota – 1889

Page 65

United States – dollar
Mexico – peso
Japan – yen
Denmark – krone
England – pound
Germany – mark
Italy – lira
Brazil – cruzeiro
Greece – drachma

Page 67

1. ankylosaurus
2. archaeopteryx
3. dimetrodon
4. diplodocus
5. hesperornis
6. ichthyosaur
7. opthalmosaurus
8. parasaurolophus
9. pteranodon
10. stegosaurus
11. triceratops
12. tyrannosaurus

Page 68

Page 70

Northern Hemisphere
Canada
China
Costa Rica
England
Mexico
Norway
Panama
Soviet Union
Spain
United States

Southern Hemisphere
Argentina
Australia
Bolivia
Chile
Fiji
New Zealand
Paraguay
Peru
South Africa
Uruguay

Page 71

1. Miners
2. Steamers
3. Skyriders
4. Knights
5. Harvesters
6. Ranchers
7. Seafarers
8. Foresters
9. Pledges
10. Winders

Page 72

1. lemonade
2. orange juice
3. apple juice
4. iced tea
5. cranberry juice
6. milk
7. soda pop
8. chocolate milk
9. hot chocolate
10. milkshake
11. ice-cream soda
12. water

Page 74

skateboard

Page 76

popcorn

Page 77

1. A comet resembles huge snowball.
2. The tail can be millions of miles in length.
3. The sun's heat melts the outer layer of ice.
4. Bits of dust and gases escape to form the tail.